How To Be ORDINARY

by
ARTHUR BURT

D0166921

PUBLISHED BY
THE EMMANUEL FOUNDATION
STUART, FLORIDA

How To Be Ordinary
by Arthur Burt

Published by
The Emmanuel Foundation
Stuart, Florida

Unless otherwise noted, all Scripture quotations
are from the King James Version of the Bible.

www.arthurburt.com

ISBN: 0-9667720-6-7

Printed in the United States of America

The Preface.
...Of course nobody ever bothers to read the Preface!

"AND AS THE VOICE COMES TO ME, so I give a decision." (*John 1:11*) Even of the Creator of the world, it's declared, "All things were made by Him and without Him was not anything made that was made." (*John 1:3, Col. 1:16*). This is an amazing Word. And the Word wasn't a word, the Word was a Person.

He divested His coat of Divinity, stepped across the stars, entered the womb of an ordinary (*ordinary*) peasant girl and became the son of man. How extraordinary!

He was wrapped in swaddling clothes in a manger—cow dung, smelly, spiders, bugs, beetles, dirt. What a welcome! Is this a revelation or a sign? (*Luke 2:12*) The Master's advent into this world, He was wrapped in swaddling clothes. Hidden, incognito. Is this revelation like the Master? As someone said, "You don't have to take lessons (*or do I?*) on being ordinary, you are ordinary!" That's the truth. Embrace it.

God is in the ordinary. Of all the "How to..." books, this one about *"How to be Ordinary"* must be at the bottom of the pile! How to Win, How to Prosper, How to be Holy, How to be Victorious, How to Overcome, How to Have a Revelation...! This is like writing a book on How to be Bankrupt! Who wants to be bankrupt?! Unlearning.

The Son of God came into the world disguised. Nobody recognized Him. "He came unto His own and His own received Him not." (*John 1:11*) Moses was raised in a palace. Jesus was born in a stable. They said of Him, "How does this man know these things having never learned?" (*John 7:15*) A workman, a carpenter. The Creator of the world in disguise.

It was He who said, "I am able to do nothing of Myself independently. I decide as I am bidden to decide. As the Voice comes to Me, I give a decision." (*John 5:30 Amp.*) This is the pattern, the pattern man.

Is this why I've missed it? I've passed by. I've been set for learning, not unlearning. I've been set for being somebody. I don't want to be nobody. Does the truth, "I am ordinary," pave the way into the extraordinary? Is this what Jesus meant when He said, "I have many things to say to you, but you cannot bear them yet...?" (*John 16:12*) Have I embraced the truth that I am ordinary?

Let me offer you a few situations that are common to mankind. Very ordinary... Who has not tip-toed out of the bedroom for fear of waking the baby, (or maybe the wife!) when suddenly overtaken by an ear-shattering, ear-splitting, uncontrollable sneeze? We all snore. We haughtily dispute it and claim we don't. I would venture to say everybody snores when they are on their back. It's very ordinary. Someone politely offers me a peppermint instead of telling me directly my breath smells. The Scripture declares, "The wind bloweth where it listeth..." (*John 3:8*), sometimes much to our embarrassment! How ordinary.

Kings and queens, rulers and dictators amazingly are as ordinary as we are. Who has not had a common cold with a runny nose? We look in the mirror and we see an ordinary person. We seek to be extraordinary.

We put in the shop window what we want to sell. But before we put it in the shop window, we adorn it, we paint it, we cut it, we adjust it, and do everything to make it appear different from what it really is. We call this pride. God hates it. I love it. Humility is an obligation, not a virtue.

Chapter 1: God Is In The Ordinary

GOD REQUIRES TRUTH in the inward parts. Now this is not an excuse to be sinful, rude or lazy. The glory of God demands reality. God requires truth in the inward parts. (*Ps. 51:6*) Not just outward. A puffing and a blowing up, padded shoulders, painted faces—everything I can do to blow myself up! I look better in uniform, so give me a uniform. Can I bear a uniform? Can I bear a peak cap? Or do I wear one to impress? The Word of God says, "Whether you eat or drink or whatsoever you do, do all to the glory of God." (*I Cor. 10:31*)

Don't we all relate to these situations? Is anything ordinary? If heart purity is seeing God in all things, *ordinary things*, I am exhorted in all things to give thanks, (*I Thess. 5:18*), then I am more than a conqueror through Him (*Rom. 8:37*) in all these things. Not after, but in them. **Big doors swing**

on little hinges Big doors swing on little hinges. A mother packs her son's lunch. An ordinary mother, an ordinary son. The result? A miracle! The five loaves, the two fishes, there's more when Jesus finishes then when He began. Did that small boy ever dream that his packed lunch would be for all mankind to read about for the glory of God?

Somebody left the gate open. Saul's father sends him out to find the asses. He never did find them. (*I Sam. 9:3*) He came back anointed King of Israel. But who would have dreamed that the gate left open would bring a situation where he would be anointed King of Israel?

Take Esther. Did she dream as a young girl, she would one day finish up as a queen? The Bible tells us about this small hinge. "On that night King Ahasuerus could not sleep." (*Esther 6:1*) That brought Mordecai in, and that brought Esther in. The strength of a chain lies in its weakest link. How strange. *How ordinary.* A sleepless night.

A wedding in Cana. No family considers a wedding ordinary. A special day. But oh, the embarrassment, they ran out of wine! When everything has to be just right. When mothers are fussing around like scalded cats, fathers running here and there like brooding hens.

And all of a sudden, Wham! "They have no wine." (*John 2:3*) These things happen. Again, it was an occasion for the Son of God. And what happened? Well, God turned water into wine.

So what is the conclusion? God is in the ordinary. And the ordinary is *extraordinary* because God is in it. "When did we see You sick, Lord? When were You in prison Lord? When were You hungry and knocked on our door, Lord? *We didn't know.*" In Matthew 25:31-46, He says, "Inasmuch as you did it, you did it to Me, and inasmuch as you did not do it, you did not do it to Me."

Chapter 2: The Glory of God Versus The Glory of Man

How do you define being ordinary? The dictionary defines it as being normal. Maybe another definition would be, living in truth or walking in truth. Truth—the glory of God, not the glory of man. The opposite of truth is pride, the glory of man, which is a lie. Pride is a huge lie.

It's an outstanding thing that God doesn't do something just for the purpose of doing it. This isn't a trite thing, it's a tremendous principle! God does not do to do. He is governed. And all that He does, He does for His own glory.

Humility is not a virtue, it's an obligation. But life is a shop window where man sells himself. In other words, he exalts himself, glorifies himself, loads himself up like a big balloon. By the glory of God, we mean the credit due to His Holy Name.

The story goes: In Dublin, a police constable found a dead horse on McConnaghy Street. He did not know how to spell McConnaghy for his report, so he pulled the dead horse around the corner onto King Street. How many of us have pulled our dead horses around the corner instead of having the truth?

The jeweler who finds the pearl of great price clears *everything* off his shelf! Did I say everything? There is one thing he allows on his shelf. It is a little black box. Possibly it would not cost as much as an American dollar. But that's allowed on the shelf because it does not distract, it does not attract. Actually, as a background, it enhances the pearl of great price and he puts the pearl in the black box. That is what II Corinthians 4:7 declares: "We have this treasure in earthen vessels, (*Why?*) **Humility is not a virtue,** that the excellence of the power may be of God and **it's an obligation.** (not, not, NOT) not of us." God is jealous. (*Deut. 4:24*)

And He is righteous in His jealousy. Everyone else is unrighteous in their jealousy, but God is totally righteous. *God's jealousy is dealing with what is totally and absolutely belonging to Him!* Man's jealousy concerns what belongs to another! Pride is a substitute for grace because pride does not recognize what it has received by grace. Pride believes it deserves what God has given, thus exalting itself above God (believing it is God) and becoming His enemy. This enhances the importance of being ordinary.

Without God we are impotent, but we think we are important. How many of us have acted important, dressed important, talked important, aimed to be important on the basis that we wanted to sell ourselves and exalt ourselves in the eyes of man?

In I Samuel 15:17, Samuel accused Saul and said, "When thou was little in thine own sight..." What are you like in your own sight? Do you see yourself as very important or what? *God does much with little, most with least and everything with nothing.* Where is the man who sees himself as nothing? The man who is little in his own eyes has a big God. The man who is nothing in his own eyes, sees God as He is. Of course, but for God, I *am* nothing. That's the truth. But do I walk in truth, do I believe the truth or do I project a lie? *"I can of my own self do nothing."* (*John 5:19*)

Our Lord Jesus Christ came into the world incognito, unrecognized, a babe in a manger. Strip this of its Christmas sanctimonious ornamentation and see it! A babe in a smelly old cow shed with stinking manure and spiders, maybe rats or mice. This is how the Savior of the world came into our planet. Unrecognized, unnoticed. And then He declared, "I can of my own self do nothing." Do I really believe that about the Lord Jesus? Independently, of Himself, He declared He could do nothing. And yet this amazing Son of Man, after declaring He could do nothing, then did everything.

So the most negative man in all the world becomes the most positive man. He heals the sick. He raises the dead. He multiplies five loaves and two fishes; there's more when He finished than when He started. The multiplication table back-somersaults! And yet, how ordinary—a working man, a carpenter. He made Himself of no reputation and took upon Himself the form of a servant. (*Phil. 2:7*) How ordinary... *how ordinary!*

They said about him, "How knoweth this man letters having never learned?" (*John 7:15*) He was an enigma. He was a problem because He was so ordinary and He made Himself of no reputation. They hinted, "We are not born of fornication." (*John 8:41*) Hinted, "This man is demon possessed, casts out demons through the devil." (*Matt. 12:24*) He took it all. Our ordinary Jesus of no reputation.

Then He says, "Take my yoke upon you and learn of Me." (*Matt.*

11:29) Do I really want to learn of Him? Do I want to follow in His footsteps? Not to speak about myself, not to exalt myself?

An amazing secret, this Savior of mine has invisible jumper cables. I was broken down on life's highway, my battery was dead. I tried pushing, but it didn't work. In despair, I stood by the roadside and along comes this throbbing, vibrant Person! He stopped. He comes where I am, the good Samaritan. I explained to Him, I had the truth, I'd broken down. He said, "It's all right. Take My jumper cables." Negative to negative, positive to positive, He applies them to me. Negative to negative, positive to positive and I'm throbbing to life! "I'm so grateful. Thank you, Oh, thank you so much! Who are you?" "Me? My name is Jumping Jesus." "Well, how wonderful! Thank you so much."

"No, no, listen—My jumper cables don't start with Me. They go back to my Father. They are not Mine. I'm connected to My Father just in the same way I've connected you to Me. And when you became one with Me, since I am one with My Father, then the power flowed to you. Understand? Well take My yoke, learn of Me. (*Matt. 11:29*) And see this, it's all in the negative. The positive needs the negative."

And I began to see something. He who has all power declares it was given to Him—given to Him! "Of Myself, I can do nothing. It's the Father that's in Me, He doeth the works." (*John 14:10*) Thine is the power. Thine is the Glory. (*Matt. 6:13*) Do you understand that? Listen! Take My yoke, take My yoke, learn of Me. (*Matt. 11:29*)

Chapter 3: "Who do you say you are?"

ALL RIGHT, from the Son of God we come to John the Baptist. Here was a man who appeared in the purpose of God. Few men have ever been questioned like he was. All men mused as to whether he was the coming Messiah. "What do you say about yourself?" *"I'm only a voice crying in the wilderness."* (*John 1:23*) He had no clothes to recommend him, no uniform, nothing in his dress, nothing in his appearance to attract men to him.

Here is this man, ordinary like his Master, a herald, but not blowing a trumpet about himself. They asked him, "Who do you say you are? Where do you come from?" And here is this man just declaring how ordinary he is.

"What do you say about yourself?" "He must increase, I must decrease." (*John 3:30*) "I am not worthy to stoop down and undo His shoes." (*John 1:28*) "A voice. That's how important I am. I've come to herald Another. I've come to declare Another." And this is John the Baptist. Quite *ordinary.* Nothing about himself, but everything to declare about Him, the coming One.

> **They were just ordinary fishermen. The world has put them on pedestals, named cathedrals after them.**

Let's look at the disciples. Peter, James, John. The record—they were just ordinary fishermen. The world has put them on pedestals, named cathedrals after them. But at the time they lived, they were very ordinary. They were squabbling as to who would be the greatest. Ordinary fishermen, mending and cleaning and fishing their nets. Peter denying the Lord, pompous, boasting, arrogant! How ordinary. Just like the rest of us. Nothing here to recommend them, just mugs, earthen vessels whom God put His treasure in.

Take anyone out of the Bible. *David.* If ever a man sunk low and had to jump to touch bottom, surely it was David. Lusting, taking a helpless man's wife, seeking to make him drunk, plotting for him to go down to his house to cover up the fact that he'd given his wife a baby. The story of Bathsheba stands out and emphasizes David was a man. He was a man after God's own heart. (*Acts 13:22*) And then to crown it all... plotting, scheming and finally succeeding in killing a man, sending a note to Joab, "Put him in the front, retreat, leave him to die." (*2 Sam. 11:15*) How despicable, *how ordinary*!

"But," you say, "is this necessary?" Well, ask God! He's the one who put it in the Book. The flaws of men have not been covered up. Truth will be shouted from the rooftop. (*Luke 12:3*) Paul squabbled with Barnabas and defeated a Holy Ghost purpose. He left purpose and entered into permission. The contention was so sharp between them. (*Acts 15:39*)

Chapter 4: But then, are there any big men?

I LIVED FOR A SEASON with an *ordinary* man that everybody thinks was *extra-ordinary*. His name: Smith Wigglesworth. Books have been written about this wonderful man. But is this the truth? Are there any wonderful men? Or is there only One who is wonderful? *...And his name is Jesus.*

Wigglesworth was a working man, a plumber. He left school when he was eight to go to work pulling turnips. When I met him at the railway station, I took his suitcases for him. My friend Jack brought the car. But Smith Wigglesworth took one look at the car and said, "What's the matter with that thing? I'm not getting in that!" Jack was a young man who had done the best he could and we'd gone to the railway station to meet the great man, who was as ordinary as any other person, and so ordinary, he wouldn't even get into God's provision. Jack apologized, "Well, I'm sorry for the exhaust smell and everything." So the big man said, "Well I'm not getting into that thing!"

So I suggested, "Well look, we can get a bus, brother, if you prefer it." And I began to explain, "There are two buses, both have the same destination on the front, Huthwaite. And we don't want the 101, we need the 106." But at that moment, the 101 drove up and Wigglesworth said, "Huthwaite!" And he stepped on the wrong bus. Well what can you do when the man of God makes his mistake? He gets on the wrong bus. All I could do was get on and pay his fare and when we got off the bus, we had as far to walk as if we'd never got on it!

That's all right for *ordinary* people, but you don't really expect great men to do things like that! *Or are there any great men?* Or do we all make our mistakes? And are we all ordinary?

Well, I slept in the same bedroom with Smith Wigglesworth. He made all the same sort of noises everybody else makes. My wife washed his clothes. Why? Because they were dirty. My friend did his finances. I don't know, could he spell? Could he write? Could he read? Could he add? He left school at eight. He was a man of the

Spirit, but he was certainly not what you'd term an educated man. I believe in later life, his wife, Polly, taught him the rudiments of reading, maybe of writing too. I think of all the hustle and hassles the people make about this so-called "great man," yet he was as ordinary as any other man.

I've seen him in a meeting and a man has come out, he responds to him, "You've been out before?" "Yes, Yes." "Go back, go back." But of course, the great man said it so you don't question it. If a little man in your eyes had said it, you'd have judged him.

He was blessed of God, wonderfully blessed of God in his ordinary-ness. For a number of years he conducted the Pentecostal Cheatham Street Easter Meetings. Impressive. It was a regular thing, Wigglesworth would convene the meetings. In one session he said, "All those who believe God is here, put your hand up." They did. "All those who believe God is going to move mightily tonight, put two hands up." They did. And God moved mightily.

But then it became a formula. God isn't a formula. *"Name it and claim it." "Confess it and possess it."* When God says it, it works. When you turn God into a formula, nothing happens. Well it became a kind of a formula.

I once saw a man come out for healing and Wigglesworth took his fist and hit him hard in the stomach. And the man doubled up. I thought, "Oh God, if that man needed healing when he came out, he needs it now!" But what do you do when the big man is in charge? When the big man says, "I'm not dealing with the sickness, I'm dealing with the devil!"

Now of course the big man said it so nobody dares to answer and nobody dares to question! But then, are there any big men? Or is there a place where all men have feet of clay, where all men at some time trespass? Is this not why we need the ministry of the Body? Is this not the failure of the one-man show that we live to the big man and dare not say anything because the big man is this *BIG MAN*. We live to him, and we dare not question him. And so his ordinariness is covered up.

Not many know that Wigglesworth, the healer (although he himself declared, "God heals, not me!") was plagued with gallstones. Jimmy Salter, his son-in-law, often had to help him to meetings near the end of his life when he'd go out with a condition of bleeding. He would go into a meeting and God would heal others whilst he himself was not healed. His own daughter, Alice, when she came back from Africa, was deaf as the result of fever. And Alice would have a huge ear trumpet, no little thing like you put in your ear today, but a fearsome trumpet that came right out and it was an embarrassment to her father. I've heard him say, "Alice!" "Yes?" "Have you got the cases? Have you got the cases?" "Faces? Who's faces?" she said. "No! Not faces—cases!" And you could tell she was an embarrassment, that huge trumpet. Maybe it was like Paul's thorn in the flesh, to safeguard God's glory.

Well, the glory of God demands not wonderful people, but the very opposite. It demands that the people who are ordinary must recognize how ordinary they are, that they might abide in Truth, which is the glory of God.

Chapter 5: "Well, fancy God moving in my old church after I left it!"

I REMEMBER A SEASON, back in 1934. I was expelled from the Church of England in 1934 because I embraced the Pentecostal teaching. I was brought before a tribunal, "Do you believe in speaking with other tongues?" "Yes." "Have you spoken with other tongues?" "Yes." "Are there any other men afflicted like you in the movement?!" And I was out on my neck! In 1934, to speak with other tongues, you were a leper without a bell! People revolted! "Ooh! Pentecostal people? Tongues people? Tongues? They roll on the floor! They spit blood! They climb the walls! They're demon possessed!" Today the glossolalia is the fastest growing denomination in the world. How times have changed between 1934 and now!

I landed in the lap of Pentecostal people and these dear people suggested until I knew what God required of my life, that I take over a daughter church from the big Pentecostal church. It wasn't a big work. It was a town in Nottinghamshire called Huthwaite. There would be about 40 people in a Sunday meeting.

Each Sunday, there was a group of girls on the back row, typical girls between the ages of 13 and 16. They laughed, they talked, they giggled. They pulled chewing gum out of their mouths and put it back in, blew bubbles, threw toffee papers on the floor and took no notice of his majesty, which was me at the other end with my open Bible, preaching my wonderful sermon. Well they irritated me. I judged them. I thought, "Give them the Word and hurl the Bible at their heads!" Now that is not conducive to anointing and I soon found I resented going to the meetings. A few weeks later, I resigned and went to London.

I was now in charge of New Southgate Assemblies of God. Out of 44 pastors, I was the youngest. And there was something almost obligatory, once a month, we were obliged to come to a business meeting. It could be defined as where a company spends hours over minutes.

At one meeting, someone brought up a reported move of God in the Midlands! Apparently a young girl, about 17, had gone up to our beloved chairman, Donald Gee, laid her hands upon him and declared that ...unless he repented of his pride, God would deal with him! Well, the heads got together, this wasn't right, this wasn't, this wasn't... "It's not correct for a female, and a young female not even 20 years old to rebuke the chairman of the Assemblies of God! How dare she!" "If it's of God, you cannot overthrow it, if it's not of God, it will come to nothing." (*Acts 5:39*) Their stand was to sit still. "Be still and know that I am God." (*Ps. 46:10*)

Well, I listened to this and decided the first opportunity I got, I would go back to my old church at Huthwaite and see for myself. The report was that God was moving there, that they were having revival there, things were happening there. I thought, "Well, fancy God moving in my old church after I left it!" I remembered the giddy girls, the chewing gum, the giggling, the lack of attention that caused me to judge them and lose my anointing and made me to move on.

The day came when I walked up to the door of the old church, the noise and the din was tremendous. I could hear it long before I got there. I put my hand on the doorknob, turned it, opened the door and it hit me, everything! Some were shouting, some were weeping, some were laughing, some were on the floor, everything happening at once! In my judgment I thought, "This is not of God." I shut the door.

I turned away and was leaving when a brother recognized me as the old pastor. He ran after me, "Brother Arthur, Brother Arthur, how wonderful to see you! Come in. Come in." I did not have the guts to tell him how I was feeling inside and I submitted to going into the church. Well I sat down, criticizing everything.

I'd only been a few minutes when Bang! Bang! Bang! on the door. The doorkeeper opened the door and their stood a big man cursing, swearing, "Give me my wife! Give me my wife!" The brother said, "She's on the floor there. I didn't put her there. If you want her, take her." I watched him go over, towering above his prostrate wife. Then all of a sudden he looked up to Heaven. From fury, his face turned to fear. He turned around and ran out of the church like a frightened rabbit, slamming the door.

I looked around, still judging everything, criticizing everything! "Oh no, oh no!" I thought, "It couldn't be! It is!" Emerging from the far end of the hall was a young girl, hands lifted up to Heaven, swaying, treading over prostrate bodies on the floor and making for me.

Lizzy Hays! Lizzy Hays—one of the girls that I had watched in the back row at Huthwaite, laughing, giggling, blowing bubbles of chewing gum, pulling it out and in, throwing toffee papers on the floor.

I thought, "You recognize me as your old pastor and now you're going to give me the treatment, the pantomime show. You'll come to me and start the business, '*Yea... saith the Lord*,' but you are not!" I remember how I felt at that moment. Almost ashamed to confess it, but I thought, "You come near me, you place your hands on me, and I'll spit in your face!" I got up and I walked around the perimeter of the hall and sat down out of sight, squinting through my fingers watching her progress. She stopped nowhere, she stopped with no one. Here she was, coming towards me. Finally she stood in front of me. I had ceased to squint through my fingers. I glared at her and I thought, "Yes, you put your hands on me," and my attitude was, "I'll spit in your face."

Her hands dropped upon me and it was an electric shock that shot through my body. Everything in me turned to jelly as if there was not another sound in the hall. I could hear her voice and she was revealing the thoughts of my rebellious heart. I cried, "Oh God, oh God, have mercy upon me."

I knew it was God. I knew it wasn't this little despised girl. I knew it was the voice of God speaking through her. And that night changed my life. I went back to London. I canceled everything and I left London and made the decision to go back to the Midlands. There was no provision for me, there was no attraction for me. I went back to nothing but the revival of God.

Tremendous things happened. The meetings often went on until two and three in the morning. Monotony, tiredness... did not exist. They belonged to a different realm. We were in the realm of the Spirit. Things that were dead suddenly were alive, pregnant with the blessing and the power of God! People were laid out all over the place helpless, laughing helplessly.

Chapter 6: He laid bare the secrets of our lives...

"OH GOD, STAY YOUR HAND! I can hold no more!" cried a visiting Presbyterian minister. He was rolling on the floor when another wave came, and another wave. People came from far and near. And the secrets of their hearts, their thoughts, were made manifest.

One night, a young woman was laid out on the floor. It was already three in the morning and we decided it was time to go to bed. Four of us went to pick her up presuming to lock the hall up, lay her on a couch and go to bed. We couldn't move her! If there had been bolts and rivets, she could not have been fastened more securely to the floor. Four full grown men could not move her! We just had to wait until His Sovereign Majesty, the Holy Spirit of God, finished His interview.

As if it were yesterday, I can see a man's head down at my foot. I was sitting on a seat and he was on the floor... rolling, struggling, fighting, the sweat rolling off him for hours, it seemed like. He struggled to get up, he couldn't. As if an unseen hand held him, he was compelled to stay until he finally settled something with God. He got up sweating, shivering, exhausted. He came to me and said, "Will you come out with me?" We went out and walked around the cemetery together, close at hand. He poured out his story.

The mission had paid for him to go to Howard Carter's Bible School in London, Hampstead. After two years, the Bible School sent him up to County Durham where he took charge of a small church. In the church was a dear man of God with three daughters. And this brother confessed that he started to court the oldest girl, got the middle girl pregnant, and fondled and trifled with the third girl. When their father discovered all this, he put his head in the gas oven and committed suicide. Then this young man returned to the mission. And all this came out as the Spirit of God dealt with him.

I saw people with their hands up to Heaven; they could not bring them down. They were fixed. Fixation of limbs seemed to be something that was much on God's program. Either they were helplessly laid out on the floor and couldn't get up, or their hands raised up to Heaven and they couldn't pull them down. I'm going back many years now, but this is the memory I have of those days.

There was a good-looking young man. Of all the young men, he was an attractive, eligible bachelor and he traded on it. He fooled about with this girl and flirted with that girl and changed to another girl. He had a beautiful motor bike. And I remember God dealing with him. In a meeting, the Lord moved upon him through a very ordinary channel. She was a slip of a girl, a nothing, a nobody, but clothed with the power of God. I can hear that voice now. "The Lord hath given thee ten minutes in which thou will either uncover or be discovered." Ten minutes later she came back and laid bare the secrets of his life. I watched him shrink.

I am not permitted to judge, but I am able to tell you that some time later he was out on his motor bike and he butterflied over the handlebars through a plate glass window. All his handsome looks were destroyed. His face was disfigured. He almost went blind. And after it, if I saw him and shouted to him, he would only respond to my voice because his sight was so impaired and so poor after what happened.

The night of Pearl Harbor is impressed upon me like a scar. We were in the meeting that night and I heard behind me, "No, No, NO!" I looked around and this young woman grabbed her belongings, pushed out of her seat, ran up the aisle through the swing doors and all I could hear was, "No, NO, NO!" ...almost screaming, as if she were being raped. Then there was a thud. I thought, "Oh God, that's her head striking the ground!"

But then I heard, "Oh yes, YES Lord, YES Lord, AMEN!" The swing doors opened, I look around. Her face was radiant. She walked down the aisle to the front of the meeting where there was a plain table and a chair, nothing else. Enacted before our eyes was something like mime or charades. But the Spirit of God suddenly came into action that needed no explanation.

The young woman picked up a mirror. Now there was no mirror there, but you knew it was a mirror. She took her hat and placed it on her head, tipped it, smiled at herself in the mirror and then turning to the company of people said, "Me, Me!" And you knew the Spirit of God was dealing with her vanity. Then I watched, she pulled out a drawer. There were no drawers there. She looked this way, she looked that way. She put her hand into an imaginary drawer and pulled out some things. She put them down into her bag by her side. There was no bag there. There was no drawer there. But the Spirit of God just clothed, created, and you knew. The people watched with a rapt attention. At the end, the Spirit of God moved her and she went to many in the meeting into the early hours of the morning, revealing their secret life.

First the Spirit dealt with her, and then, as the Spirit had His way, He used her in her nothingness to reveal the thoughts of people's hearts. You may find it in the scriptures, "The secrets of men's hearts being made bare." (*I Cor. 14:25, Ps. 44:21*) You may remember things in the scriptures like Ananias, or Gehazi, the servant of the prophet, and other instances where God revealed men's secrets.

Chapter 7: Now the amazing thing was... He did it with nobodies.

NOW THE AMAZING THING was He did it with nobodies. I saw how the Spirit of God clothed ordinary people almost like blowing a balloon up, especially if you've ever seen a balloon in the shape of an animal or a person. Then as the breath goes into the balloon, it rises up into whatever shape the breath would produce inside it.

We had nights and nights of meetings going on until one and two in the morning. This was in a town where children had to go to school; men had to go down to work in the mine. It was a direct invasion by the sovereign Spirit of God.

One night, a pastor stood up and announced, "Tomorrow night, we'll close the meeting at nine o'clock. We'll have an early night." The following night, he stood up, announced the meeting was closed, walked up the aisle and opened the door at the back. And the Spirit of God came into such an ordinary girl, Lizzy Hays. I saw the Spirit of God lift her out of her seat, transforming her. Like a queen, she walked up the aisle, confronted the brother who had announced the closure of the meeting, touched him and WHAM! Down he went! ...laid out on the floor. With all the supreme majesty of a queen, she raised her hand, and looking down at him with supreme scorn, I heard her say, "Wilt thou, WILT THOU limit the Holy One to one small hour?" She turned around and she walked back like a queen in all her majesty, took her seat and became ordinary Lizzy Hays.

This went on for weeks and weeks and weeks. God would pick this young girl up and use her in all kinds of ways. It had been rumored that she walked up, put her hands upon Donald Gee, the Chairman of the Assemblies of God and said, "Thou art a proud man and unless thou doest humble thyself and repent, the Lord will deal with you." For six weeks, Donald Gee submitted and trembled under that Word. Then he was persuaded by others, "Who was it? A slip of a girl?! A teenager?! A female?! How dare she rebuke the leader!" Finally he was dissuaded and as far as I know, rejected the message. I'm not sure about that, but as far as I know.

The meetings continued in the Midlands. People came from far and near. The supernatural was there. Time stood still, stopped the clock. People had visions. They cried out, some of them ran out.

One woman unwisely stayed until the meetings finished, one or two in the morning. Her husband was the postmaster in the village. He was unsaved. Obviously, he judged his wife coming in at one and two in the morning. He judged that she was involved with somebody up at the mission. And instead of in some measure seeking to win her husband by her conversation, that's how the scripture puts it in I Peter 3:1, she found herself locked out. I think she had to sit in an outside hut or toilet or something because her husband locked her out and refused to let her in. She had nowhere to go so my wife and I made room for her at our house. Then he spread it through the village that I'd stolen his wife.

He was storming and raving about those fanatics at the mission! One night, the door at the mission opened. He came in. I was sitting at the front with two other brothers. He had a gun and he was drunk. He staggered down and came and cursed me, pointing the gun at me. Obviously he didn't shoot me. Obviously he didn't kill me. He cursed me by everything he could. Then he walked out the back door of the mission and he got a can of paraffin, and set the place on fire. We'd asked God to send the fire, but we didn't mean it as literally as that!

Accusations were scrawled all over the mission. The windows were threatened to be smashed in and things got very, very, very dangerous. They usually do. "All who desire to live godly in Christ Jesus will suffer persecution." (*2 Tim. 3:12*) Persecution is God's income tax. Little income, little tax. Big income, big tax. No income, no tax. Well we proved it in those days. God was moving and so was Hell. The meetings continued. People came, people went. God continued to move.

Who was this little girl, Lizzy Hays? She was the outstanding one that God used again and again. People fell under the power of the Spirit, the secrets of men's hearts were revealed and all through a little slip of a girl, a nobody, Lizzy Hays.

Her mother was dead, her father rented out the rooms of his house to Indians selling silks. And Lizzy was put in for an extra pound or dollar a week. She was put into anybody's bed who was prepared to pay the price. She was bullied, she was threatened by her father who took the belt to her and made her poor skinny little body black and blue. Despite that, when God touched her, every opportunity, she was at the meetings. I remember a time when we had to hide Lizzy. She was pregnant by one of these men and he came to claim her. She didn't want to go and we had to hide her. The man came for a number of weeks before he gave up and left her alone.

She continued and then an amazing thing began to happen. Although she was nobody, although she was just a thin little waif of a girl not twenty years old, being wonderfully used of God, it seemed as if she couldn't bear it. The time came when Lizzy began to think she was the meeting. Rather than seeing that the Spirit of God was the only supreme operator in the meeting, she saw how she was being used and slowly it began to creep up on her, "Well, this meeting doesn't begin until I come into it."

The Spirit lifted off her and picked up one or two others in the meeting and the same outstanding ministry was demonstrated. God visited! She couldn't bear it. She became offended. Slowly but surely things changed. Before she died in December 2002, I visited her many times in an old people's home. She was in her seventies. When I talked to her about those days, she just said, "Did I? Did I? DID I?" God seemed to have erased from her memory every trace of the visitation. Every trace. She went out into normal Christian circles and joined a mission somewhere else. She moved out and moved on and God safeguarded His glory and erased from her memory every trace. She became a little old lady, so deaf you had to shout to make her hear your words. And she had no memory of the past. None!

Chapter 8: Pride, the enemy of God's glory!

LET'S PURSUE THIS SUBJECT of being ordinary, which actually means being in truth. Because the truth is, *I am ordinary*. I am, just in the accepted sense, normal. I haven't arrived, but I have left.

May I present an alternative to why we have so little when God has promised us so much? All right, I've been a Christian over 70 years. I've done all the accepted things. Prayed all night. Fasted from food, the mirror, swimming, many other things. But I'm still faced with an issue, this question. Why have we got so little? Why does the bag have holes in it? The Lord Jesus mentions about bearing. Bearing.

May I offer this as we pursue? Is it because we cannot bear that we do not have? This issue is wrapped up in a sentence I often repeat. "If you can handle it, you'll have it; if you haven't got it, you can't handle it." That's the plain elementary truth. Who would give a ten-year-old child the privilege and responsibility of sitting in the driver's seat and holding the steering wheel of a vehicle? The child could be killed or kill others.

May I offer this? The answer comes along the line of being ordinary and having the truth of being ordinary. Everybody is ordinary whether they believe it or not. But how many people really believe they're ordinary and betray the fact by seeking to be extraordinary?

We're all seeking to increase rather than this issue of decreasing. John the Baptist saw this. "He must increase, I must decrease." (*John 3:30*) This was what John the Baptist saw.

God is jealous and righteous in His jealousy. He will not give the credit or the glory to another. (*Is. 42:8*) There is a fierceness about the jealousy of God. Of Him are all things. Of Him are all things. (*Rom. 11:36*) We have sought to get out of being ordinary. You are ordinary whether you believe it or not!

> "I haven't arrived, but I have left."

Now this damnable thing that God hates, pride, man's glory, aims to fight God's glory. It is the enemy of God's glory! It is the rebellion of the creature against its Creator!

Pride corsets the flesh like a woman who wears a corset to appear what she's not. The corset pulls the flesh in, as in the days of Queen Victoria when ladies wore corsets. Wealthy ladies would have a maid in the back who would pull the laces in. She'd put her knee in the lady's back, pull it tight to give her a wasp-like waist. Could this be the reason Victorian ladies fainted so often? Could be! They pulled the flesh in. It was deception. They appeared thinner and trimmer than they were. There is a corresponding imitation of this whereby pride pulls the flesh in, makes it appear it is not there.

But pride is a many-headed monster. It is not only like a corset, it's also like a balloon. If it suits its purpose, pride will blow a thing up far beyond what it should be. What happens when a child's balloon is blown up so tight? It doesn't yield and the end can't be tied to keep the air in. Whoosh! Off it goes! Or if it can be tied, the tiniest prick... Boom!! Up it blows!

Well we've seen a lot of people go off. Pride either keeps the flesh in or blows the flesh up. It varies between puff and crush. If I can't be the hero, well all right, I'll be the villain. But I must not be ordinary. Whatever happens I must not be in that position where nobody notices, nobody takes any notice... they pass by my shop window and never even look in. My pride demands that you stop and shop with me.

Notice the things that are often the evidence of people's pride. Maybe not always, but they can be breeding grounds for pride. Earrings, wigs, bras, sneakers. Not all of them, or all the time, but many of these things, and more, are the outward evidence of an inward condition where people want to be noticed. They magnify themselves, the way they walk, the way they talk, how they dress, all these things can be evidences of this one thing, pride.

"I want you to know I am not ordinary." I like to vaunt myself with my degrees: M.A., B.A., D.D., X.Y.Z., anything you like. I want you to know my title. "I'm a Pastor." "I'm a Prophet." "I'm an Evangelist." "I'm an Apostle." Can I hold what God has given me to the glory of God or do I use it to demonstrate, "I am NOT ordinary." Do I wear my police uniform or my business suit to the glory of God, or do I use it to bully you, vaunt myself, strut, crow... or like a peacock, spread my fanned feathers? Only God knows. Motive is something unseen that governs the why that governs the what I do. Do I hold what I do to God's glory or to my glory? Do I recognize that my God is extraordinary, but I am ordinary? The disciples squabbled behind the back of Jesus as to who would be the greatest. Jesus took upon Himself the form of a servant, He humbled Himself. (*Phil. 2:8*) The natural man does the opposite.

Behind what I do is always the motive why I do it. The motive is like the motor in your car. It's the driving force. It's the impelling force that makes you go forward, fills your shop window, governs not what you say, but why you say it. That's the motive. You tell a story, I'll tell a better one. You've been here, you've been there, but I've been here, I've been there. And always, there's the desire to excel, the desire to outdo everybody else.

Chapter 9: Becoming as little children... in the humbling, the simplicity, the transparency.

Now this thing is so subtle in us that it often swings into reverse and we seek to be proud of our humility. And we're too cunning and too clever to be as naive as a child who obviously will artlessly boast. Take the artlessness of kids. "I'm bigger than you are!" "Yes, but I'm more clever than you! Look what I can do! You can't do what I do!" They are backed to the wall of lying. "You can't play. I'll not be friends with you. I'll take my ball back home, so there!" "Well, my Daddy's a policeman and he can lock your Daddy up! So there!" "I'm not friends with you!" Out comes the trump. "You are dirty, you smell." The artlessness of children is revealed in simplicity, in truth and without pretense. There's no pretense.

An important visitor comes to the house. Little girl looks at him to the embarrassment of her Mummy or her Daddy, "We've got lice. Have you got lice?" The important visitor looks shocked. "We get time off school. The nurse comes and we don't do any lessons. The nurse goes hunting for nits in our heads. It's fun. We get away from lessons. Isn't that nice? Have you got lice? Oh no! You wouldn't have lice. You've got no hair!" Much to the embarrassment of the parents!

The rent man comes. Mother says to little Johnny, "Tell him I'm out." Little Johnny goes to the door, "Mum says she's out!" The ordinariness, the artlessness of the little child. No wonder Jesus says to become as a little child, (*Matt 18:4*) to become the simplicity.

The preacher is roaring from a built-up pulpit above the platform. A little girl clutches her daddy's arm and as the preacher waves his arms and shouts and roars, the little girl says, "Daddy, will he hurt us if they let him out?" We smile at the simplicity of a child.

"Daddy, why don't you have a lot of hair? Why do you not have any hair on the top of your head?" "Well, you see Daddy's brain does a lot of work and it wears all the hair away. Daddy's so clever he's lost his hair." "Oh." Afterthought... "Daddy?" "Yes?" "Why has

Mummy got such a lot of hair on the top of her head?"

We educate our children, encourage them to be extraordinary. They finish up by considering we are hypocrites, we are proud, people-pleasers, and yet, we tell them not to tell lies.

Looking at things through the window of a child's mind, becoming as little children, not necessarily being little children and never growing up, but becoming, in the humbling, the coming down, the simplicity, the ordinariness, the artlessness, the transparency. Jesus is utterly transparent! He is the Truth. (*John 14:6*) Philip said, "Show us the Father." (*John 14:8*) Jesus said, "Philip, have I been so long a time with you? Have you not seen Me? If you've seen Me, you've seen the Father." (*John 14:9*) In other words, if you've seen Me, you've not seen Me, you've seen the Father.

Take a clean sheet of glass or a window. If there is no grease, no steam, no grime, no dirt on the glass, it's just as if it isn't there. And when you look, you don't look at it, you look through it. If you look at it, it's because there is something on it. But if there's nothing, then you look through it. You see the trees, the flowers; whatever is beyond, you will see. You look through it. When we are ordinary we are living in truth. Truth is transparent and so is the window of a child's mind. We don't see the glass, we see through the glass.

Consider a child's mind. This little fellow's in his crib. What does he do with himself? He sees something between his legs and he begins to fiddle with it and he's told, "That's naughty, you mustn't do it." All right, he looks around. He sees an odd piece of paper and his little fingers play with it, he pulls it, and off comes a piece of wallpaper. Again he's told, "You are naughty, you must not do that!" Two or three weeks later, Daddy and Mummy come up to the bedroom armed with scrub brushes, scrapers, buckets and they don't pull a little piece off. They strip the walls completely off! Somehow the child has to grasp in innocence the difference between innocence and ignorance.

Notice little children are sweet until they know they are sweet. Then they are no longer sweet. All they did in innocence, they now do to impress and this thing is fed inside of them, the tree of the knowledge of good and evil. God says if you eat you die. (*Gen. 3:3*) How good is the knowledge of good when God has forbidden it?

Chapter 10: Not what I do but why I do it!

THE SCRIPTURE TELLS US TO "Beware of philosophy..." (*Col. 2:8*) Beware of philosophy. One could add at this point, God doesn't need your wisdom but He can do without your ignorance! Don't put a premium on ignorance. There's a fine line where you find that the bath water is dirty and you throw the baby out and you throw the bath out. But there's nothing the matter with the baby! There's nothing the matter with the bath! It's just the water that was dirty.

It is so easy to go from one extreme to the other and pride is so subtle. If it can't glory in being extraordinary, it will wear the garments of ordinariness and glory in being ordinary. To everything there is a balance.

Stiletto heels, shoulder pads, spectacles... Why do I have spectacles? To see better or to look intelligent? Why do I have a beard or why do I not have a beard? A mustache, lipstick... There is a subtle psychology about these things. Not what I do but why I do it!

Hitler was a little man. He was nearly always found in uniform. To impress, he had a command room with a long corridor leading up to it and the room was high up. By the time anyone got to the room where Hitler was, he was looking down at them. They were being psychologically brain-washed and they were being made to know who was the boss.

When I was a boy, I did a bit of boxing and I had a tooth broken. Then I slipped in another boxing match and another tooth broke off into Eddie Rowan's leg. He had to have my tooth extracted from his leg. Then I fell out of a tree, somewhat flattened my nose and broke a third tooth. Here I am with three broken teeth. I thought, "Well, I'm ugly." So I developed a habit to never laugh. I don't—to this day, I don't laugh. It's habitual. I smile, but I don't laugh.

It goes back to those early days when I would stand in front of the mirror, keeping my top lip down as I spoke or as I preached. I didn't have dentures until I was 19. I would watch my top lip covering my broken teeth while I was preaching, "God loves you my friends!" I wasn't bothered about whether God loved them, I was concerned about my broken teeth, covering them up, trying to look something that I felt I wasn't. I would present the left-hand side of my face always to people, hide my three broken teeth on the right-hand side. I didn't chase girls. It wasn't that I didn't like girls, but I felt that I was ugly. What girl would want me? So my hurt pride took over until I had dentures.

When I was in Paddock Wood we had an arrangement there. I was pastoring there for twenty years along with a brother, Archie Friday. We would often take turns preaching at the Wednesday night meetings. One Wednesday, I drove a bus load of children to Folkston for a day's outing by the seaside. While I was in the sea, a huge wave hit me and knocked my dentures out of my mouth. I crawled on the sea bottom holding my breath whilst feeling around to find my dentures. I couldn't find them. I came up and I drove back to the church, everybody teasing me, joking. "Ha! Ha! He lost his teeth," they laughed.

That night it was my turn to preach the Wednesday night meeting. I said to Brother Archie Friday, "Would you change places with me? I've lost my teeth. It would be a day or two before I could get fresh dentures made." He turned to me and said, "You're always preaching about pride, now get on with it and demonstrate it! It's what you are without your teeth." So that night, I had the great privilege against my ego of preaching without my dentures. He was quite right. It did my pride good. But my pride isn't there to be good. My pride shouldn't be there. But then, beware of philosophy. We're not recommending people sit on the toilet with the bathroom door open. No, no! Beware of philosophy!

Chapter 11: Johnson's at the door: Body Ministry

I THINK OF THINGS that just show how ordinary I am. As far as I know, the rest of me is real except as someone said, "How can you preach truth through false teeth?" I now find, at 92, I'm forgetting a lot of things. I got out of a car a while back, undid my seat belt and found I didn't have it on. I suddenly discovered my trousers were around me feet. "Ha,Ha! Ha! Ha!" Everybody had a laugh. Well that's how ordinary I am! I haven't even got my seat belt on. I undid the belt to my trousers.

When I was a boy, I kissed a girl and she fainted and I ran away thinking she dropped dead. When I go out into the garden in winter time and come down the hill, I often find I'm unaware I've got a drip on the end of my nose.

We have an arrangement at our house. It's called, "Johnson's at the door." A dear lady, wealthy, who often had a drip on the end of her nose, made an arrangement with her butler. She said, "Now Jeeves, when you see me with a drip at the end of my nose and I'm in company, and I'm talking to people, just say, 'Madam, Johnson's at the door,' and I will immediately know what you are saying and I will remedy it." One day the good lady was talking and the drip came. Jeeves said, "Madam, Johnson is at the door." She didn't hear. "Madam, Johnson is at the door." She still didn't hear. "MADAM, JOHNSON IS IN THE SOUP!" Well, we've introduced that into our mode of living here. I happen to be the guilty party, the one who needs reminding, "Johnson's at the door."

My eyes are not too good. Thank God I can see! But I sometimes miss a soup stain and sometimes I need a reminder, "Johnson's at the door." So now it's developed into part of our lives. I'll say, "Is Johnson at the door?" It's part of 'Body Ministry'. I need other people. I do! I need them! And I'm grateful.

Have you ever considered that when someone offers you peppermint, that maybe your breath smells? Well, you're ordinary. Consider it. This brings us into a new dimension, Body Ministry. What do we mean by Body Ministry? Well we've been emphasizing that you are nobody. But is that the end of the matter? Do we wallow in self-pity? Do we sit under an eternal juniper tree having pity parties? "I'm nobody." Or rather, do we see the glorious possibility of what God can do with nobodies? Does it not say in I Corinthians, do you see your calling? Well, do you? Do I? "That God hath chosen the weak things, the base things, the foolish things, the despised things and the things which are not." (*1 Cor. 1:27*) The nobodies.

The Word of God says, "Do you see your calling?" (*1 Cor. 1:26*) Every negative statement emphasizes that I am nobody. This does not put me out, it puts me in! I am part of this Body that God has purposed to use for His glory. (*1 Cor. 10:31*) Whatever problems there are with the one-man ministry, cease to be in the revelation of the Body. The only Person in the Body is our Lord Jesus. He is the Head of the Body. The glory is safe with Him. But now that God has delegated, distributed, spread abroad ministries, He thereby seeks to safeguard His glory. He placed a flaming sword to keep the way of the Tree of Life. (*Gen. 3:24*)

God has protected His glory. He is fiercely protective and jealous of His glory. He will not give it to another. (*Isa. 48:11*) He guards the glory. The Bible uses a word in the Old Testament for glory, *Chabod*, which has to do with weight. *Ichabod*, the glory has departed. We are not interested in it departing. We are concerned with how to invite it and for it to come. And it shall only come, conditionally, related to the credit due to God's Name.

Can one man bear a ton? Can 20 men bear a ton distributed into 20 hundred-pound weights? This is the question! Jesus says, "I have many things to say to you, but you're not able to bear them." (*John 16:12*) Bearing is introduced. Bearing brings in the issue of God being glorified.

In the human body we've got an eye, an ear, a foot, a lung, a kidney, an elbow, a knee, an ankle—all part of one body. Here is the wisdom of God. The glory of God is likened to the distribution of members in the body. For instance, the eye has a function to see, the ear has a function to hear, the foot has a function to walk. The foot can't see. The eye can't walk. They are faced with an issue of safety to the glory of God. They can't. But together they can, under the Head.

Remember the Church was birthed at Pentecost when they were all together. Jesus has prayed that we may be one just like He and the Father are one. (*John 17:11*) The members need one another to function. How can the eye see unless the foot directs it into the purpose of God? How can the foot walk except the eye sees where it should walk? In a healthy body, every member is ordinary and normal in its function.

You can never exchange the member's function. You can't walk on your ears. You can't talk with your elbow. Yet the elbow plays a tremendous function when the hand is holding a cup. And with all the bending of the head, the easiest way is for the elbow to function and bring the hand up to the mouth. This is the elbow's function. But who wants to talk with their elbows or walk on their elbows? The elbow's helplessness emphasizes its function. Each part is only able in line with its function, which is enabled through the other ministries in the body. The knee bends. The ankle, the elbow, etc.

Each member's function deals first with the glory or the credit due. A member's function is totally unable, except in order. Order is vital to the ordinary man. He may not be extraordinary. He is purposed to be ordinary in order. That means the hand will handle. The mouth or the tongue will speak, the eye will see, the ear will hear. This is purpose.

Do you see your calling? God has chosen you! You don't have to be something you're not. You simply have to have the truth of what you really are! You're *ordinary*.

Chapter 12: I can of mine own self do nothing...

DIVINE PURPOSE is using ordinary people who recognize they are ordinary and will not seek to be extraordinary. Man fails by aiming to be what he's not. He can only be effective in his function. And he will discover his function by the unction on his function. In other words, the will of God works. But the will of God is meant to work perfectly with ordinary people who realize they are ordinary and, as such, will not move out of order. All our troubles come in exalting ourselves. We trespass out of our function and aim to be what we could never be, because God never meant us to have any function outside of what He gives us. *Selah!*

One Head is the Head. The Head of the Body is our Lord Jesus. Amazingly, He declares, "I can of mine own self do nothing." (*John 5:30*) I am being compelled by circumstances all my life to believe this.

I don't believe it, therefore, I have to prove it. I arrive helpless, useless, like a car with a flat battery. *(I know this was in Chapter 2, but I've been delivered from the fear of repetition. It's important— read it again)* I've tried pushing, I've tried pulling, I've almost ruptured myself, but I can't start it. Ah! Here comes somebody. I've flagged them down. "Could you help me please?" "Of course I can." And this person puts jumper cables on my flat battery, positive to positive and negative to negative. The Son of God becomes the Son of Man.

The negative is vital. That's the whole purpose! I need to be positive about the fact that I am negative. Now that is the revelation of God. God is positive for the negative. Do you see your calling? God has chosen you! You don't have to be something you're not. You simply have to have the truth of what you really are! You're ordinary. You are very ordinary. When I cease trying to be something I'm not, then God comes into my life.

Now the power is throbbing through my poor flat battery! Now my life is throbbing with power! How? I look to this Person. He takes the jumper cables off; He puts them away. I say, "Thank you!

Oh, thank you, Sir, so much! What is your name?" He says, "Oh, my name? It's Jumping Jesus." "Jumping Jesus?" "Yes!" "Oh, how wonderful! Well thank You for giving me a jump!" He says, "You don't understand, do you?" "Well tell me."

He explains, "My cables don't start in me. Just as I connected you to My cables, My cables at the other end were connected to My Father. Don't you see that? When you become positive with your negative, then you'll find the power will flow. Take My jumper cables, take my yoke and learn of Me. (*Matt. 11:29*) Do you see it? I am like you, a flat battery. I can of My own self do nothing! It's the Father that's in Me, He doeth the works. (*John 5:30*) But He only does those works because I am connected to My Father. I am totally helpless of Myself, but I am perfectly fulfilled in being plugged in or connected to My Father. He does the works in Me. Now understand this! Come here! Let Me talk to you."

"All I ever did, I never did. (*John 5:30*) All I did, I didn't! I did not do what I did do. Do you understand this? I am a flat battery connected to a throbbing Father by jumper cables. Do you see that? Only when you are positive with the negative will anything positive ever come out of you. You've looked in the wrong place and you've not had the truth. You are bankrupt! You are a failure! You cannot do anything!"

"Why should you think you are better than Me, the Son of God? If I can do nothing of Myself, (*John 5:30*) who are you to think you could do something of yourself? This is the root cause of all your failures. Like it or not, you think you're better than I am! You're not! You're not! Don't you see, smoldering inside you is a volcano ready to erupt at any given moment. How do you erupt? In your judgment of other people—all of a sudden you erupt when you meet another individual."

Now the next thing is the uncomely member (*1 Cor. 12:23*) in the Body. Is there such a thing? I know the scripture declares it. But maybe God is looking through the window of my attitude toward another person. In terming someone else uncomely, have I not seen I'm revealing what I believe about myself? I declare your ruler isn't straight and put my crooked ruler against your ruler. What's revealed? It's my ruler that isn't straight!

Romans says, "Thou that judges doest the same things." (*Rom. 2:1*) Things that irritate me are the things I am guilty of. Thou that judges doest... I'll either believe it or I'll prove it.

So now, I judge. In the Body, there are uncomely members. Some members in the Body are so uncomely in our estimation, we do not even like to talk about them. But how did you get into the world? Did you grow on a gooseberry bush? Or did your father and mother rub noses? Well you know the answer to that. We are very, very ordinary people and we need to adjust to God's standards instead of ours. There are no uncomely members in the Body except one and that is me. I am ordinary.

But when I embrace the truth of this, I see that God has put more abundant honor on the uncomely member. This is where God's glory is safe. We have this treasure in earthen vessels. God deposits in somebody who is so totally unattractive. They are like the little black box that holds the pearl in the shop window. Nobody considers it beautiful or attractive. Nor does it distract. It's a background for the glory of the pearl. No one notices the box, their eye is on the pearl. There is only One who is wonderful and his name is Jesus!

> ## There is only One who is wonderful and his name is Jesus!

No one sees the clean window, they see the magnificent view through the window. What a wonderful thing when people will not see me, but will see through me and see God. To see through you and see the altogether lovely One! What a triumph of grace when others will not see the earthen vessel, but the glory it contains, the altogether lovely One. This is the purpose and the plan of God.

Chapter 13: The goal of God.

THE BODY IS ALSO TEMPERED. "Huh! He lost his temper!" And we look upon temper as if it was some kind of graspable, grabable thing that could be held, dropped, hurled or lost. Steel is tempered as it yields. We must recognize that members of the Body must be tempered; they must have the ability to yield and have no desire to operate outside of their function.

There is no jealousy on the keys of a good piano. When the musician touches, it goes down; when he lifts his finger, it comes up. There is no jealousy or envying with the black notes or the white notes on a good piano. They are totally inanimate, helpless until the musician touches them. Here is a picture of the Body—no desire to be in, not hurt when I'm left out. This is the normal ordinary life, or should be, of a believer.

What is the difference between a boxing match and a football or soccer match? In a boxing match, one man knocks the other out and gets all the glory, all the credit. In a soccer match, it's teamwork. The team is only effective if they recognize one another and work in order. No jealousy, no desire to exalt oneself. The man who keeps the ball and dribbles down the wing with it and keeps it will soon be out. Maybe the center-forward is in the best position for scoring the goal. But unless somebody passes the ball, how can he score a goal? And when he scored the goal, how could he have scored unless someone gave him the ball? So somebody has to learn to pass the ball and keep sweet when the center-forward scores the goal. This is teamwork. There must be no seeking for position, no projection of self. Eleven ordinary people recognizing that their effectiveness is as a team and not on their own.

In a soccer match, the goal is the goal. It doesn't finally matter how pretty your teamwork is and how wonderful you may show up on the field, the ultimate is the goal. Not the teamwork, however pretty it might be, or however fancy it may be, but did you score a goal? That is the ultimate, the goal. And the result is how many goals each side scored.

"Oh, the work was pretty! You should have seen the artistic..." It

41

doesn't matter, you're not there to show off. You are there to score goals. And as in the natural, so also in the spiritual.

What is the goal of God? His glory, the glory of God. And the glory of God is related to what? My being ordinary! My being ordinary! Surely we need to see that this is what the divine Coach seeks to produce. Not talk, not show, but goals. And the ultimate goal is that the credit, the glory, goes to God. Anything less, anything else is waste. "Thine is the glory..." (*Matt. 6:13*) It is the ultimate goal of life.

A little boy was an orphan. His foster parents adopted him. He went to school. Children can be very cruel. They picked on him, they teased him. "You don't have a real Daddy! You don't have a real Mummy! You are an orphan! You have been adopted!" One day the little fellow was sitting on the steps crying his eyes out as the children cruelly teased him. Then he turned and he said to them, "All right. I am adopted. My Daddy and Mummy came to the orphanage and they picked me out of 400 other little orphans. Your dads and mums had to take what they got!"

Well, of course, there is something in seeing through the window of a child's mind. But, the revelation of God is that He didn't choose me because I was extraordinary. While we were yet sinners, so ordinary, Christ died for us. (*Rom. 5:8*) So ordinary. I have nothing to boast in! So ordinary. He passed by and He chose me. I'm just an ordinary sinner.

> Nothing in my hand I bring,
> Simply to Thy cross I cling;...
> Rock of Ages cleft for me,
> Let me hide myself in Thee.
>
> (*Rock of Ages, Augustus M. Toplady, 1776*)

Chapter 14: How many in the Church, are spiritual freaks and don't know it?

L ITTLE CHILDREN ARE SWEET until they know they are sweet. Then they are no longer sweet. This is a process that applies to us all. We cease to consider we are ordinary and we move into thinking we are extraordinary. This thinking is the breeding ground of pride and it grows unconsciously like a tumor or parasite. It is fed by success, and the consciousness of being ordinary ceases. Innocence makes way for ignorance. Humility is lost in pride.

Consider again the image of the human body. Obviously if I have a 15-foot arm or I have 40 eyes, I am not ordinary. I would be a freak. Apply this to the Body of Christ. If I have a ministry outside of my function, an over-extended ministry, I am not looked upon as a freak, I am looked upon as wonderful. Extraordinary! But have I trespassed on your ministry?

When I was in Niagara Falls, I went over to the Guinness Museum to see the extraordinary at the lunch hour. And I met a woman with a claim to be the biggest woman in the world, I've forgotten whether she was seven feet or 7'9". There she was, nobody was there except me, a quiet time. She was living. By her side was a television.

She opened up to me and mentioned how her young brother had to do her shopping. He was 6'10". She shared with me the tragedy of her life. She could not drive, she'd no hope of a family, a husband, she was looked upon as a freak. And she told me how for many years she was in such hurt pride.

"Then," she said, "I felt like I had to embrace the situation. It was the only place I could get out of pain. I was so miserable and so wretched to be an object, to be looked at by the public. The doctors tell me I have no expectation of life beyond 30 years of age. My knees are so painful I can barely walk. I sit, I knit, I watch television. That's my home life. This is the only way I can earn a living. I am treated as an object of amazement. I am a curiosity, a freak. In some measure, I've adjusted to this."

I talked to her and found her very open to conversation. She spoke about the Lord and I spoke about the Lord and we shared.

I came out and wondered how many in the Body of Christ, in the Church, are like this poor girl. Poor, but they don't know it. At least she knew it. They are spiritual freaks and don't know it.

They not only fulfill their own function or ministry, but they encroach on other people's. They are extraordinary. Or so they think as they boast about "my ministry" when, in truth, they're trespassing on your ministry. I believe every member has a dormant function in the Body of Christ. "Neglect not the gift that is in thee." (*1 Tim. 4:14*) How many people who are being passively entertained in the Church have slumbering, latent, neglected gifts?

So many meetings are like spiritual concerts. A number of professionals entertain. A dozen people on the platform will dominate in the meeting whilst the rest are only spectators. They are not participators, which is the divine plan—to become, in the perfection of the plan, "...to the measure of the stature of the fullness of Christ." (*Eph. 4:13*)

The Church doesn't seem to see it, and you get the big one-man show. Or maybe you get a big 10-man show! The whole thing becomes kind of a spiritual concert, a religious show. I've even been in meetings in Texas where the congregation will clap after those on the platform have finished their performance. How sad. How we fail to see that these people are bordering on being spiritual freaks. They are like the man with the 15-foot arm or like the man with 40 eyes. Anything beyond two is an extreme and they are extraordinary. Anything beyond the acceptable length of an ordinary arm makes them extraordinary. And they are really spiritual freaks, that's all.

This can cause offense, of course. Truth always does. How many meetings could you go into where you can say to the people, "Have you come here to watch the freak show?" They would be horrified. But is this not the issue? Most people attend a meeting with neglected ministry lying dormant within them. They are only there to watch. They are spectators, they are not participators.

Test what I'm saying. Does not the Word of God say or demand, "Neglect not the gift that is within you." (*1 Tim. 4:14*) If you don't use, you lose. If you want to develop, don't neglect exercise. How many people are in a spiritual limbo because they don't get any exercise? Now we have seen it in the physical. But have we seen it in the spiritual? Neglect not the gift that is within you. The Spirit divides to every man as He will. (*1 Cor. 12:11*) Does He not come to you? Does He only come to me? Am I a superior being? Or do you have a ministry? And would your ministry develop more if I shut up more? Oh dear!

Chapter 15: How important is order?

$\mathcal{S}$TAND UP, speak up and shut up. How many people in full-time ministry have never learned to shut up? They have lost sensitivity when to sit down and let the Spirit move other people. Read Ephesians 4 again. Uncover, discover your hidden ministry.

In a jig-saw puzzle, every piece is essential. And I cannot fulfill, or therefore, fill full my ministry except your piece goes into place. I may not be able to function until your piece begins. Then my piece makes sense, and we are made perfect in one. Here is perfection. Not in one piece, but where is my zig? Fits your zag. I need your zag for my zig. And together we are made perfect. (*John 17:23*) Here's perfection. Don't be afraid of it. We are made perfect in one. (*John 17:23*) I need you. You need me. We are ordinary people who need each other. The perfection of the saints comes about with ordinary people.

Let's have a look at this word ordinary again. Let's split it. The word 'order'nary... ordinary. Sounds almost the same, doesn't it? 'Order'nary. Ordinary. But you will read ordinary. How important is order? How much does order take its importance in ordinary? Consider this. How important is order? Look at your telephone, a bunch of numbers, but they're meaningless except they are in order. Your call doesn't go through unless the phone number is entered in order. Your car spark plug wires, 1,4,3,2 or 1,3,2,4, are not the same. If you get your wires wrong you are ineffective, the car won't go.

Every member of the human body enables the body to live in health if the members are in order. Even the mighty ocean submits in order to the function of the gravity of the moon and can be forecast when and how the high tide will come. An old bewhiskered salt with a big peak cap and a blue jersey writes on the board of the promenade, "High Tide, 10:42". The seasons—spring, summer, autumn, winter. How can you reap in winter? How can you reap in spring? You bow to the order.

Of what value is a "naught", a zero, a nothing? Well you could say it speaks for itself. A nothing is a nothing. But an ordinary naught, zero, in its right order, under the governing factor is tremendous.

And the ordinary becomes extraordinary when it is governed and subject to order. Thus, the pound sign (or dollar sign) plus one, the unit, or the naught (zero) before the pound sign, before the unit, is meaningless. It is out of order. But in order, after the governing factor, the pound sign or the dollar sign, then the unit. And then in order, the naught or zero adds value to the unit in order. It is $10 not 0$1.

The scripture says the head cannot say to the feet, "I have no need of you." (*1 Cor. 12:21*) In the wisdom and economy of God, the Lord Jesus needs you and needs me, the ordinary nobodies, to value and to declare the glory of God. Isn't that wonderful? "His strength is made perfect..." (*2 Cor. 12:9*) His strength is perfected through my ordinariness, through my weakness, which does not draw away or distract from His value. The glory is God's as my glory is absent. How many choirs sing, "Glory to God" but never humble themselves?

Consider Elijah. In James 5:17, it's declared that Elijah was ordinary. He was a man subject to like passions. Elijah didn't consult the weatherman when he decreed, he declared, he delivered and he demonstrated, "There should not be dew nor rain... but according to my word." (*1 Kings 17:1*) How tremendous, how wonderful! The zero in its right place becomes so powerful. The ordinary, governed, becomes extraordinary. Fire comes down from heaven! (*1 Kings 18:38*) And yet the man is so ordinary that he runs away from a woman! (*1 Kings 19:2*) How extraordinary.

I now begin to see how handling is married to having. I will have what I can handle. But if I can't handle it, I won't have it. Who would allow an eight-year-old to sit in the driver's seat with his hands on the steering wheel and the engine running? Surely this would mean death, maybe death to the child, maybe death to passing traffic. However much the child may beseech Daddy, "Let me drive, let me drive, let me drive..." All the importunity in the world which could avail in another time in another place would be completely out of order here. No amount of importunity would ever allow the child out of order to drive the vehicle.

Elijah, after the event, after he'd run away from a woman who had threatened him, (*1 Kings 19:2*) sat down under a juniper tree and had a pity party. He was so ordinary. "I am not better than my fathers." (*1 Kings 19:4*) Well who said he was? Where did he get the idea that fire coming down from heaven was related to himself rather than related to God's glory? Surely, in the light of the Holy Spirit, an ordinary man slipped into hurt pride and prayed that he might die. Yet the answer to his prayer was in Jezebel who vowed, "May the gods do to me and more also if I make not thy life like the life of one those prophets that you slew." (*1 Kings 19:2*)

He lands up in a cave. The Word of God comes, "What are you doing here?" "What doest thou here?" (*1 Kings 19:9*) How extraordinary. The man who seemed so mighty, slaying 450 prophets and bringing fire down from heaven, somehow got tangled up in the situation. And like so many, he didn't know how the sovereignty of God and human responsibility operated. What will God do because I can't do it? And what will God not do, because I must do it?

If I am not defined on how ordinary I am, I touch God's glory and then God touches me! In His jealousy, He will not give the glory, the credit, to another. Only with the ordinary is divine power safe. But the ordinary has to recognize how ordinary it is. We are all ordinary, we are all earthen vessels. But how many recognize that the treasure within is not of me, not of us? This is the danger. This is the place I can cease to be a steward. "Thine is the glory." (*Matt. 6:13*) The treasure is not, not, not of us. We are all ordinary. But do I believe it?

In Acts 14, the apostles came and the people said, "The gods have come down to us in the likeness of men." They put garlands on them. And the apostles tore their clothes, ran out, and in effect, they said "Don't do this! We are ordinary, we are like you. We are men, like you. We are not gods. We have done this through another

The sovereignty of God and human responsibility... What will God do because I can't do it? And what will God not do, because I must do it?

power, the power of a Name. We are ordinary men operating with an extraordinary God. Thine is the glory!"

In Noah's day, God repented of making the earth. (*Gen. 6:4,5*) Men had become mighty. Men had become men of renown. (*Gen. 6:4*) They no longer saw themselves as ordinary. What did God do? God saw their pride and destroyed the world in a flood. At a later date, He brought down the Tower of Babel and cursed men with different languages. (*Gen. 11:1–9*) See the jealousy of God against anyone who exalts themselves, anyone who does not realize the order of being ordinary?

Chapter 16: The entrance back into my birthright is to humble myself to the truth. I am ordinary.

IN EZEKIEL 36, the Lord declares, "In the day when I put My Spirit in you, you shall loathe yourselves. Remember that you were slaves and I didn't do it for your sakes. I did it for My Name's sake. And you will loathe yourselves in your own sight." Now we're not called to snivel and go about all the time sniveling. But at that time, "When I put My Spirit in you, then remember. Remember, remember... then is the hour to loathe yourselves!" Now that was the Old Testament declaration. God said, "In the hour when I bless you, you must in your own sight remember you came from Egypt, remember you were slaves. In your own sight, see yourself as very ordinary."

Now, in the New Testament, it changes. The revelation is different. It's not loathe yourself, it's lose yourself. I cease to be an entity. I cease to be another. I cease to be a target for the jealousy of God. He will not give the glory, the credit, to another.

The revelation is now the Body, which is the Church. In the Church, there is only One. Our Lord Jesus is the Head of the Body. We lose our identity in the revelation. I'm in.

I need to know what my function is when I am in. Am I a knuckle, a knee, an ankle, a liver, a kidney, an eye, an ear? I need to know my function. I need to recognize it. There will be unction on my function. But there will be no consciousness of myself. Self-consciousness goes in the presence of God. God-consciousness overwhelms as much as the rising sun eliminates the glory of stars at night. How many stars do you see when the sun shines? Not one.

All right, you may contradict what I'm saying by reminding me of Isaiah who said. "Woe is me, I am undone, I am a man of unclean lips." (*Isa. 6:5*) This was his only consciousness of himself. Not a recommendation, but a recognizing of how ordinary he was. How extraordinary.

When the prodigal came home, the words he put upon his lips were, "I am no more worthy." (*Luke 15:21*) He never was worthy!

Worth is related to birth. Even when his worth was measured in pig sludge, he was still a son. A prodigal son, yes, but it was at that point, in the depths of despair, he realized how ordinary he was. "I am no more worthy." And at that point, it registered. He decided, "I'll go back to my father." (*Luke 15:18*)

When you know that you are ordinary, you have got to wait. If you have no car, you wait for a bus, you wait for a train, you wait for a friend to give you a lift. Important people hate to wait. They also hate to be kept waiting. You must wait for them. "They that wait upon the Lord shall renew..." (*Isa. 40:31*) Ordinary people must wait.

"If you do not consult Me, you insult Me."

Only emergency or important vehicles, like the fire brigade, an ambulance or the police do not have to wait at traffic lights. Do I run before God? Because I am ordinary, I wait for the plane. At the set time... Wait... Be still... (*See Gen. 21:2; Is. 40:31; Ps. 46;10*) God has rebuked me again and again by saying, "If you do not consult Me, you insult Me."

The entrance back into my birthright is to humble myself to the truth, I am ordinary.

God's normal man, our Lord Jesus, declared this truth in John 5:30. "I can of mine own self do nothing." How ordinary. How useless. How helpless! He is the most negative man that ever lived. But He now becomes the most positive man that ever was!

"Worth is related to birth."

After acknowledging He can do nothing, He then does everything. He stills the storm. He raises the dead. He heals the sick. When He feeds the multitude with almost nothing, five loaves and two fishes, there's more when He finishes than when He started. He turns water into wine.

What does He mean? "I can do nothing." But He qualifies it, "...of mine own self." (*John 5:30*) Then He calmly declares, "It is the Father that dwelleth in me, he doeth the works." (*John 14:10*) Do I believe this? Do you believe this? All Jesus ever did, Jesus never did. The glory is God's.

Chapter 17: What will it cost me to buy the truth?

THE PERFECT PLAN is to make an incomplete man. God's ways are not our ways. The incomplete man is an ordinary man who knows he's ordinary and has the truth he's ordinary, believes he's ordinary, and then watches God as an eyewitness. God loves me. So in the purpose of God, the only way into the extraordinary is through the ordinary.

Because man has never grasped this, never believed this and never wanted to believe it, the extraordinary has been barred. The flaming sword (*Gen. 3:24*) to most has been a complete mystery. It turns every way to keep the way to the Tree of Life. It bars the way. Could this be the way? By being ordinary, which is the truth of what I am, the Spirit of God who alone exalts the Word of God, who is our Lord Jesus, can guide me beyond the flaming sword! Like a field mined and full of danger, and yet it is possible with a guide to cross the field. Only the Holy Spirit can take mankind back into the garden. Why? He knows the pitfalls, He knows the lies, He is the Spirit of Truth. And He can guide you and guide me back into our birthright.

On what basis? Well, on the basis that I now see being ordinary in a new light. In the revelation of God, I see it, not as preventing me, but inviting me and purposing to lead me back into my birthright. I now see that this word "ordinary" means truth. It is the truth, I am ordinary. And as I embrace the truth, it makes me free. (*John 8:32*)

I see the Word of God is likened to fire. And I believe that the Word of God will try every man. Once I have come through the fire, the fire has left ash and gold. Ash can't be burned, gold can't be burned. Gold, He says, "I counsel you to buy of Me, gold tried in the fire." (*Rev. 3:18*)

So as I choose the glory of God, that all the credit is God's and none of it, none of it, no, none of it is mine, the Spirit of God can take me and bring me through the flaming sword. I believe the flaming sword is the Word of God. "His Word was like a fire shut up in my bones." (*Jer. 20:9*) But I've already met the Word of God, I've already met the fire, or have I? Only as the Word of God burns up the wood, the hay, the stubble and the rubbish, (*Isa. 5:24*)—only then can I proceed back. And the Spirit of God can lead the people of God beyond the flaming sword. The Sword of the Spirit which is the Word of God will try me and burn up my rubble and leave me with nothing but gold.

Now until I've gone through this fire, I'm not ready to go through the next fire. After the fire, a still small voice.... (*1 Kings 19:12*) This is the record spoken about Elijah. After the fire, a still small voice. After the fire, the Spirit. Then the Spirit can take us by the hand through the flaming sword.

Once the Word of God has dealt with me in fire and burned up my rubble, my rubbish, my wood, my hay and my stubble, what have I got to be afraid of? What can the flaming sword do to gold? Once the Spirit of God takes me and leads me back to the flaming sword, I see the possibility of being back in my birthright.

I have to buy the truth. "Thy word is truth." (*John 17:17*) What will it cost me to buy the truth? My wood, my hay, my stubble, my Ishmaels... my pride, my pomp, my vanity. This is my rubble, this is my stubble and this is my rubbish. How pathetic that I cling to this lot and I'm not prepared to trade it for the gold of God, which is the glory of God.

I now begin to get some sort of an adjustment. I begin to see God's mind about being ordinary. I am ordinary. I am the earthen vessel. I'm the weak man. I can of mine own self do nothing. (*John 5:30*) Are there any other words in the Book that can so completely express my ordinariness as these?

I have had the world's attitude to being ordinary. I have sought to lift myself up. I have sought to exalt myself. I have sought to sit on the throne instead of being subject to King Jesus. Christ shall rule in your hearts. (*Col. 3:15*)

I now see this revelation of my ordinariness as a tremendous possibility, an invitation that there shall be from this a demonstration. If I am not willing to demonstrate my ordinariness, will I ever be ready to demonstrate God's extraordinariness? Am I not a danger to the glory of God? Am I not a target for the ruthless jealousy of God who smites the Uzzahs (*2 Sam. 6:7*), brings insanity to the Nebuchadnezzars (*Dan. 4:33*), and smites the pompous, arrogant Herods arrayed in royal apparel with worms and curses? (*Acts*

12:21–23) Is this not the truth? I believe it is.

I now see the value of being ordinary. And when I am, it's only the truth. And the truth makes free (*John 8:32*) and the truth is the glory of God. We're back to the beginning where it all began at the foot of the cross. And what did we sing?

> Just as I am, without one plea,
> But that Thy blood was shed for me,
> And that Thou bidst me come to Thee,
> O Lamb of God, I come, I come."
> *(Just As I Am, Charlotte Elliott, 1835)*

Chapter 18: How many lives are out of order?

THE HUMAN BODY. Every member enables the body to live in health if the members are in order. The sea can be forecast when and how the high tide will come. The seasons: spring, summer, autumn, winter. How can you reap in winter? How can you reap in spring? You're bound to the order.

Timing, punctuality, computers—all meaningless except they are governed by order. "Out of Order" is a dreadful phrase. "Out of Order" spells Disaster! "Out of Order." Do you get it? OUT ...of order. Does it matter? Of course it matters! There is an accepted time. Now is the accepted time. (*Eccles. 3:1*) Esther, you've come to the Kingdom for such a time as this. (*Esther 4:14*) Time dictates order. What is discord? Music out of time, music out of tune, music out of order—it isn't music, it's discord.

Does order matter in competition? Well of course it does. One horse wins the race. Another horse also ran. One team scores three goals. The other team scores two goals. Does it matter? In the Olympic race, he who comes in first wins. Does it matter? Of course it matters.

On the road, traffic lights dictate and we bow to an order of stopping or going. If you break that order, you'll do more than break the order! Road signs—the circle commands, the triangle advises. If you break the law, you find out that the law breaks you. There is an order. The quickest way downstairs may be through the bedroom window, but the order is down the stairs. The quickest way may delay you for six months on a hospital bed. Of course order matters. Of course!

The river flows. Water finds its own level. It bows to an unseen law called gravitation. Now this order begins in heaven. The Father is number one, God. The Son is number two. He says, "My Father is greater than I." (*John 14:28*) He also declares a total loss of identity with dependence. "I can of My own self do nothing..." (*John 5:30*) The Holy Spirit, number three, is dedicated in lifting up another. One, two, three. That's the order. He is subject to the Son. "When I go, the Comforter will come. I will send Him." (*John 14:16*) The Holy

Spirit was not yet given because Jesus was not yet glorified. (*John 7:39*) The pattern begins up there. One, two, three.

I need to see the pattern. I need to bow to it and see how vital it is to be order-nary... order-nary. Only when I am order-nary, do I understand what it means to be ordinary.

Sickness in the body, the body is out of order. The big word is malfunction. Arithmetic is meaningless. My sums are wrong unless they are in order. Spelling demands letters in order. Presumption and anticlimax—both are in disregard of the governing factor, which is order. How many meetings have no recognition of divine order? How many meetings do not recognize the principle, "The Spirit divides severally AS HE WILL." (*1 Cor. 12:11*)

How we grieve the Spirit of God by not recognizing Him. Could you do this with a traffic light? Could you go when the traffic light is red? Well, of course not. Beginning before God begins is presumption and continuing after God has finished is anticlimax.

Abraham's mistake produced Ishmael. Isaac is purpose, Ishmael is permission. According to Ecclesiastes 3:1–8, there's a time for everything, a time for this, a time for that. Time is the governing factor and if it's recognized, it produces order.

"If you're full of yourself, you've no room for God."

I need to recognize order because I'm ordinary. And of myself, I don't know. And I need to recognize somebody who does know. For instance, a child runs to his Daddy. "Daddy, there's somebody at the door." "Daddy, somebody wants you on the phone." Daddy responds to the voice of the child and may even run to obey. But that same voice can be rebuked if it is out of order. The same voice that would want to dictate when we go out, when we come back, whether we go to a meeting or whether we don't, that voice is now out of order. It has to be ruled, because it is unruly. It is now inordinate, out-of-order.

How many lives are out of order? Their god is their belly or their god is the garden or business or money or pleasure or the television. These things can be acceptable in order. But once they are out of order, they become idols and God becomes my enemy because of His jealousy. Men are exhorted in the Word of God to love their wives. But once they make an idol of their wife and put their wife before God, then their life is out of order.

Of course, the function of the human heart, the hidden man of the heart, is to believe. I either *believe* in my heart or I believe in my *heart*. What is the difference? Well I can believe God in my heart, which is the function in order. Or, if my heart dictates and

Ordinary...

Order-nary. Selah.

enters the throne, instead of believing God, it becomes a god so that I believe my heart, and it's out of order. My heart is now dictating; it is now reigning. Instead of Christ ruling in my heart and reigning (*Col. 3:15*), I now find that my heart needs to be reined in.

Chapter 19: Living by a Proceeding Word.

MANY YEARS AGO, I often visited a family in a little place called Knotts-End beyond Fleetwood near Blackpool. My friend Bob worked on the ferry boat there. I would get on the ferry boat and look down at the engine room to see if Bob was on duty, whether he was on early or the later shift. If he was on early shift, the engine room would be open. The heat was tremendous. I'd look down and say, "Hello Bob, I've just come to see you and Emily." "Oh, that's fine, I'll be off at five o'clock, Arthur."

Then I'd watch. I'd stand there and see the captain go on the bridge. The river was very busy at Fleetwood and lots of boats would be coming down, mostly trawlers going out into the North Sea fishing. The trawlers went directly out of the river, whilst the ferry boat went across the river. I observed that the communication between the captain and Bob in the engine room was governed by a series of rings, kind of a bell. One ring might mean start, two rings, half speed, three rings, full speed. Four rings might mean slow down. Five rings might mean stop. I can't remember the exact order of the order. But it was vital! The boat would pick up speed, the boat would be at full speed, or the boat would stop in mid-river according to the number of rings communicated from the captain to Bob. There was complete unity between the captain who could see and Bob pulling the levers down in the engine room.

Jesus is my Captain. He sees, He conveys by the ringing of bells, by my Spirit. Go. Slow. Stand still. Stay. Go. God has rapped my knuckles many times and said to me, "If you do not consult Me, you insult Me. Your life is out of order."

What sort of a man am I? Am I an ordinary man? Well am I an order-nary man? Being order-nary involves having nostrils. If I do not have nostrils, I'm not an ordinary man. Why did God give me nostrils? Where there is air, I live. Where there is no air, I suffocate. Suffocation means death. An environment means life. The environment I need is air. We all began life in the womb. Then we were birthed into a new dimension. We wait. The midwife waits for the first cry of the baby as it takes its first breath in the new environment. Otherwise, it is stillborn.

To breathe is ordinary. To breathe is normal. To breathe is natural. Spiritual existence parallels the natural. I live out of the mouth of God. God breathed, man became. God is still breathing and man becomes.

The lungs of a drowning man are filled with water. It is a foreign substance. He was never made to live without breathing. So the first thing is to get the man out of the water. The next function is to get the water out of the man. We call this artificial respiration. You cannot fill a full vessel. The first thing is to empty out what should not be there.

When I was in Michigan, I was eating some coconut pie. A piece of coconut got stuck in my throat and I could not breathe. I was strangled, I couldn't gasp. I was at the point of suffocation. A man saw my situation and getting behind me, he put his two arms around me and punched me in the stomach. And I honestly believe he saved my life! I could not live without breathing. Neither can you.

Being ordinary involves having nostrils, whereby air is conveyed to the lungs. And thereby a process of in-out, in-out... we live. It's ordinary to breathe. It's normal. It's natural. In the natural, there is a process of out-in, out-in, out-in and there is a parallel in the spiritual. Man should live a normal life, an ordinary life by breathing God in and expelling anything that goes against God. That should be living by a proceeding Word. (*Matt. 4:4*) Heart purity is seeing God in all things. (*Matt. 5:8*) Not some things, all things. This keeps my whole life transparent, seeing God in all things.

The devil has lost his nostrils. He lives by bluff, dependant upon your believing. What you believe rules you. He is involved in deceiving and accusing. Once you believe a lie, he rides in on the lie. He is powerless in truth. Jesus says, "All power is given unto me." (*Matt. 28:18*) At Calvary, the power of the devil was destroyed. (*Heb. 2:14*) But you and I often give back to the devil what Jesus took from him! The devil tricks us into doing this by the artificial, by imitation, by bluff, by deception, by lies. But then, whilst he may fill his shop window with these goods, he needs me as a customer. If I don't go into his shop, he continues in his bankruptcy, powerless.

But he sets the window. He makes a show. Then I go in and

"What You Believe Rules You."

give him back what Jesus took from him. Calvary means just that. According to Hebrews 2:14, our Lord Jesus became one of us and through death destroyed him that had the power of death, that is, the devil.

Fear is the imitation of faith. Fear is the substitute of faith. Just as faith goes into the Word, which is truth and becomes creative, fear goes into a lie and becomes creative—if I receive it! Fear is believing the devil's lie. Faith is believing God's truth. The devil in truth is powerless.

Chapter 20: Our Environment is Vital!

Environment is vital. Take the shark. In his environment, he has power. That vicious jaw, those rows of knife-like teeth can snap an arm off! But if the shark is out of his environment, let's say he's not in water, he's in a car park, a parking lot. He is surrounded by Chevrolets, Fords, Mercedes... out of his environment! That vicious jaw cannot go down and snap up and cut my arm or leg off. He's tossing, turning, struggling, fighting, not against me but for his very own existence.

In water, his environment, he is fierce, dangerous. Out of his environment, he is totally inoperative. I don't get too close, but I look at him and watch him. And all his efforts are struggling against the wrong environment. He cannot live. He cannot continue. He cannot survive, just as the devil lives not in the truth (*John 8:44*). The truth defuses his bomb. The truth paralyzes his efforts. The truth makes inoperative everything he has because he only works in deception. The shark, out of his environment, out of the water, is powerless. And the devil in truth is powerless.

The bird needs the air. Those wings are trapped in a cage. It has no sky, it cannot fly. The plant needs the soil. Everything needs an environment. I do, you do. In the natural, we must have air. In the spiritual, we must have His Spirit. Thus, we can lead a normal life in Truth.

The Spirit of God is the Spirit of Truth. (*John 14:17, 15:26, 16:13*) God's ordinary man must walk in truth. And that makes him normal. A miracle is a miracle among people who are not normal, but subnormal. In the land of the blind, the one-eyed man is king. But if God visits the land of the blind and gives light and sight to the blind, then the blind man sees and the one-eyed man is no longer king. He is no longer on the throne. He's lost his position.

If I am breathing exhaust fumes, carbon monoxide, I am taking on board poison, death. Try holding your breath. You can't do it. If you don't breathe, you'll die. It is a divine order that I must submit to. If I am an ordinary man, I must submit to the process of out-in, out-in, out-in. Whilst it may be ordinary, it's absolutely vital.

Consider climate. Climate allows an ordinary man to do extraordinary things. Can you grow an onion? Can you swim? Camp out? Fish? Travel? Sow? Reap? All these things are governed by climate. Climate provides the environment. God says, "It's not by might, nor by power, but it is by My Spirit." (*Zech. 4:6*) "I dictate through My Spirit. I release through My Spirit." That which has been bound in ice and snow is released by a change in climate.

I enter into another realm, transferred from darkness to light. (*Col 1:13*) The birds wing to the sky. Man breathes to life, living in truth in the realm of the air. Reality, normality, being ordinary, walking in the light (*1 John 1:7*), hating darkness—this is the purpose of God. Darkness does not fight light, it flees from it.

Chapter 21: "Under..."

IN PURSUING THE SUBJECT of being ordinary, we come up against the word inordinate. Inordinate means excessive, or out of order. If it is inordinate, it is not ordinary. I go to the dictionary. I find it easy to locate it in the dictionary. Why? Well I get an ordinary dictionary, and in two minutes I find its meaning under the "I", inordinate. I don't have to struggle for hours, the dictionary is in alphabetical order. I won't find inordinate under "A" or "C" or "Q." I find it in order under "I" for inordinate.

What does the word "under" convey to me? Well it conveys a lot! I think of the centurion in the Bible, how he said to Jesus, "Speak the Word only, I also am a man set under authority." (*Matt. 8:9*) So an ordinary man is set under authority. This centurion had to submit to Caesar. Well they all submit to Caesar. They all say, "Caesar is Lord!" They have an obligation to put themselves under. If they don't, they lose their heads. But Caesar knows the difference between a man who is just under tradition and the man who, from his heart, puts himself under the authority. Under. Under....

I am ordinary. I am an ordinary subject of the Queen of England. I am under her authority. She doesn't even know I exist, unless I defy that authority. If I throw a brick through the window at Buckingham Palace, then she would notice me. She doesn't know that Arthur Burt exists. I'm ordinary. I'm ordinary because I am a subject. I'm one of millions of subjects, which means I recognize authority and being subject, I'm under.

Now Moses said, "Who am I?" Well I am a subject, I am under. Out of being under, Caesar put the centurion over. In other words, the centurion's authority came out of his subjection. If you are too big to be led, you're too little to lead. He's now able to say to this man, "Go," and he goes, "Do this—" and he does it. Why? Because he is set over, because he put himself under. That's the principle.

> **"If you are too big to be led, you're too little to lead."**

67

Chapter 22: The Secret of Samson was the Spirit of God.

M OSES SAID, "Who am I?" (*Exod. 3:11*) The great I Am said to Him, "I Am that I AM." (*Exod. 3:14*) This brings in a tremendous issue. We are now moving from the ordinary to the extraordinary, from the norm to the abnormal. Moses said, "Who am I?" Well, who was Moses? He was a poor preacher, slow of speech, not eloquent. He was not a man of words in the natural. Why do we know about Moses? We know about him because he was able to bear God acting through him, able to bear God's power without taking the credit.

Our land is full of powerless preachers. With all our preaching, it's been pitiful, the lack of power that we've had. You remember the Word, "Tarry until you be endued with power." (*Luke 24:49*) Ordinary fishermen, endued with power! Well they were ordinary! Peter could curse with the best of them. They could quarrel like silly children as to who would be the greatest. (*Mark 9:34*) They were ordinary.

Consider Samson. Was he ordinary or was he extraordinary? This man comes onto the stage of life and the first thing recorded about him is that he was extraordinary. He wasn't ordinary. That's why Delilah said, "Tell me your secret. Tell me your secret." (*Judg. 16:6*) Now the secret of Samson was the Spirit of God. It wasn't a machine gun. It wasn't that he carried bombs around with him. He lived in an ordinary way, an ordinary life, but manifested extraordinary power. "Tell me your secret. Tell me..."

The Spirit of God came mightily upon Samson. The secret of Samson's strength was the Spirit of God. You see it in the Book of Judges. Every time he did something in consequence, it came out of cause, the Spirit of God. This was his secret. Now this meant Samson was not some huge man about 6'10" with bulging muscles and legs like tree trunks. If he'd been like that, Delilah would not have needed to say, "Tell me your secret." But surely, it was a secret. A man who could slay a thousand men, not with a gun, not with bombs, but with the jawbone of an ass! (*Judg. 15:15*) How ridiculous! What would you say today of a man who killed a thousand men with a coat hanger?

That's bringing it up to date. What power is there in a coat hanger? What power is there in a jawbone of an ass? None. Can you conceive? A thousand men were slain by one man! How could any ordinary man have done that extraordinary act? Surely there was a secret, but we know the secret. The Word of God tells us it was the Spirit of God. (*Judg. 15:14*)

Therefore, the Spirit of God can transform ordinary people. On what basis? Well, with electricity, you plug into the power and you switch on. Then the power flows through. Now with this, very much the same situation, by plugging into Truth, the ordinary man becomes extraordinary. Truth being the dominant factor of the Spirit of God who is the Spirit of Truth. So power comes through walking in truth. How much truth have you had? In line with the truth, you plug in and you switch on. But can you avoid the truth that you are ordinary?

Now initially, the Spirit of God came on this ordinary man, Samson. He was so ordinary, he was an immoral man. He wasn't a virtuous man. You can't say the Spirit came upon him because he was a good man. This blows away all your conceptions of theological understanding. The Spirit of God came on a man who was immoral. He was going with harlots.

Now I have to do some adjusting. The Spirit of God can use an immoral man. Well have you ever been used by God? Have you done everything you should have done? Did you think God blessed you because you were you? Did you not know who you were? Had you forgotten that Moses said "Who am I?" And the great I Am said, "Forget it! It's not who you am (pardon the grammar), it's who I Am."

Chapter 23: God does much with little, most with least and everything with nothing.

So now comes fresh truth. The Spirit of God comes first on, before in. There is an initial invasion of every man where the Spirit of God comes on. It has nothing at all to do with the man. God invades him, directly touches his spirit and he's plugged into power.

But if he thinks that he'll continue, he has another *think* coming. Whilst it is initially on, it's to be permanently in. What's the difference? Truth has to be bought! At first, you see truth, you acknowledge truth. The acknowledging of truth prevents me from going out, but it does not put me in!

I'm like a woman passing by the shop window. I see the goods, I acknowledge their value, but they are not mine. The next thing, I see a ticket on the goods, there's a price to pay. So then I make a decision either to buy the truth or to pass on. Now if I decide to buy the truth, I next go to the counter. And it's there at the counter that I buy the truth.

Now when you've paid the price, it's in. It's no longer on. Your revelation is married to the situation. The counter is the situation. The shop window is your revelation. You see it. It's on you. And initially, that's God. Then comes your responsibility where you have to buy what you see.

Now when you've paid the price, it's in. It's no longer on. Your revelation is married to the situation.

In doing this, you are like a man taking a photograph. You capture the scene either in the sunshine or with a flash. The result: you've got a negative. And that negative is the opposite of what you wanted. Your negative has to be developed in the dark. The initial light is gone. You captured it there. But now it is upside down. "Now it's the opposite of what I wanted. I don't want this! I'll tear it up, I'll throw it away!" No, no! Treasure your negative.

Have I done this? Have you done it? In the dark, which follows the light, the heart has to believe what the spirit saw. Your spirit saw it; your heart now, in the dark, must believe it. There are no windows. I used to tell the story about your heart, which is like the *'fella' in the cella*." Your spirit was up at the top of the house in the attic. If your heart falls out with your spirit, your heart calls your spirit, *"That fanatic in the attic!"* But when the light comes on you, you have the privilege of it being in you when your heart believes what your spirit saw.

You develop your negative and you bring it out of the darkness into the light. Your heart has to conjure up, ruminate like the cow, regurgitate like the parakeet, and bring back again what you saw. As you bring it back, then it is fixed! Where is it fixed? You come out of the darkroom to a tank of acid and you put your negative in it. Somebody will always supply you with the fixer or the acid, don't worry! But then you have your positive. It's no longer on, it's in. God does much with little, most with least and everything with nothing.

John the Baptist saw it. It was a gradual decrease, which is the price you pay for God's increase. How many emphasize fullness, but never seem to recognize fullness depends upon fullness of emptiness first? Except you surrender, and surrender is not surrender unless it is unconditional. Emptied out, "Lord, I surrender all." It's no good talking in terms of Ananias in keeping back part of the price! (*Acts 5:1–5*) You keep back part, you'll have a part-salvation. You surrender total if you seek for a total salvation. So God does much with little, most with least and everything with nothing.

Where is the man who is so ordinary, that in his assessment of himself, he sees himself as nothing? Nothing. We sometimes ask the children, "What gets bigger the more you take from it?" It's a riddle. Of course the answer is—a hole. The more you take from a hole, the bigger the hole gets. The more God takes from you, the bigger God becomes in your life. If you're full of yourself, you have no room for God. But if you are going to follow the revelation of God, you're not only going to seek to be ordinary and become as a little child, (*Matt. 18:3*), but you'll stay there! The man who is little in his own eyes has a great God. But the man who becomes nothing in his own eyes knows God as He is.

This is the revelation of the Body. I have no identity, I have no personality in the Body. The only one in the Body is Jesus, the Head of the Body. I am simply a member, I am not a somebody. Therefore I'm delivered from the jealousy of God who will not give the glory to another. Am I another? Are you another? Or is there only One? And that is Jesus, the Head of the Body!

Book Orders & Information

Web Page: *www.arthurburt.com*

E-mail: *foundation@arthurburt.com*

Or write:
The Emmanuel Foundation
39 N. River Road
Stuart, Florida 34996
USA

Books can be ordered in the U.K.:
Arthur W. Burt
"Bron Wendon"
Conway Road
Penmaenmawr, Conwy
LL34 6 BB
North Wales, UK

Other books by Arthur Burt include:
Around The World In 88 Years
The Silent Years: A Divine Apprenticeship
Boomerang: The Funeral Of Failure
Surrender: Your Key To Spiritual Success
Cock-A-Doodle-Doo
Pebbles To Slay Goliath